Big Cat Mysteries of Somerset

CHRIS MOISER

Bossiney Books · Launceston

Other books by Chris Moiser

Mystery cats of Devon and Cornwall
Mystery sea serpents of the South-West

Some other Bossiney books about Somerset

About Glastonbury
Ghosts of Somerset
Introducing Exmoor
Legends of Somerset
Mysterious Somerset
Shortish walks on Exmoor
Traditional Somerset recipes
Visions of Glastonbury

The cover is a composite picture of a puma in Newquay Zoo (photo by Mike Thomas) and Cheddar Gorge (photo by Paul White)

First published 2005 by Bossiney Books Ltd
Langore, Launceston, Cornwall PL15 8LD
www.bossineybooks.com

ISBN 1-899383-78-6

Acknowledgements
The map is by Nick Hawken. The photographs are reproduced
by kind permission of Gillian Dale (pages 7 and 23),
Mike Thomas (page 9) and Paul White (page 11).
All other photographs are by the author.
Printed in Great Britain by R Booth Ltd, Mabe, Cornwall

Introduction

Although most of the sightings of exotic large cats in the United Kingdom are associated with Devon and Cornwall or Scotland, there have in recent years been a large number of sightings of these mysterious animals in Somerset.

Such animals are called 'exotics' by biologists because they are not native to Britain, or at least haven't been native in recent times, and for this same reason some people refer to them as 'Alien Big Cats' or 'ABCs'. Alien in this context means that they are from another country, not that they are extra-terrestrials. Locally they tend to have other names such as 'the Bridgwater Beast', 'the Beast of the Blackdown Hills' or 'the Shipham Panther'.

The word 'beast' to describe wild cats probably originates from the use of the phrase 'Beast of Exmoor' which first appeared in the late 1970s and early 1980s. The problem with the 'Beast of X' type names is that the UK is a relatively small country, and most wild cats have large ranges. The Beast of the Blackdown Hills one night could have moved into the Quantocks by the following morning.

In considering the existence of these animals most people will probably want to know how they came to be here. The simple answer is that we do not know. Several possible explanations exist. Some are more credible than others and some receive much more publicity than others.

1. Survivors from the prehistoric past

The leopard or panther is supposed to have become extinct in Great Britain by the end of the last ice age, about 12,000 years ago.

Traditionally the lynx is said to have gone the same way before the Romans arrived, typically some time in the Bronze Age or Iron Age. However a few lynx bones found in Scotland were recently dated as being from about AD 180. This suggests that small numbers hung on for longer than was previously thought.

The puma is an American cat and has never lived in Britain, except possibly for the odd escapee from captivity.

The chance of a population of lynx or leopard, whether black or spotted, having survived virtually unnoticed to the present day seems highly unlikely. It's thought that the European wild cat disappeared in Somerset in the 19th century, although being less noticeable some may have remained until much more recently.

2. A species unknown to science

This again is highly unlikely unless a form of hybridisation has occurred, i.e. a crossing between two species. Hybrids are usually sterile, but occasionally in the cat family some do occur which are fertile. The classic example of this is the 'Kellas cat' found in parts of Scotland; it's a cross between the European/Scottish wild cat and the domestic cat.

Recently hybrid cats called 'Bengalis' have been imported and subsequently bred in the UK; these are crosses between domestic cats and Indian leopard cats. The objective in producing them was to create an animal with a domestic cat temperament and the spotted coat of the leopard cat. Other hybrids have been produced in captivity in the United States to get around legislation that controls the keeping of wild animals.

3. Released from captivity, either intentionally or accidentally

This could have occurred in a number of ways, and at many different times. The oldest possible releases could be the offspring of escapees from travelling menageries in the late 18th century onwards. Escapees, however, were commonly reported and generally lions and tigers were either recaptured within 48 hours or shot.

A typical example of this happened at Queen Camel, 8 km north of Yeovil, in the 1890s. The lion bolted when the door of its cage was opened for the trainer to enter. It ran away and sheltered in an outhouse from where it was subsequently driven back into its cage – the cage having been placed next to the outhouse door.

The lion that escaped from Anderton & Haslam's menagerie when it was at Martock was not so lucky. It attacked the menagerie elephant and was shot to prevent it from further harming the elephant or escaping again.

Smaller cats that escaped may not have been recaptured or reported for fear of claims for compensation when domestic livestock was subsequently killed and eaten. Escapees in the 1960s and 1970s were most likely to have been from private collections or the many small zoos that disappeared during the economic recession.

The explanation that the press seems to like best is that a number of exotic cats were deliberately released in England and Wales when the Dangerous Wild Animals Act 1976 came into force. Many owners, faced with a prohibitive charge for inspection and licensing, had to dispose of their animals. Rather than have them destroyed they turned them out into the countryside. It's a neat theory. In January 2000 a retired 'lion-tamer' in Birmingham claimed he had released leopards and pumas in Derbyshire in 1974. Interestingly it was not a criminal offence to liberate exotic species into the wild until 1981.

If a number of animals were released, it seems likely that they would have been seen on a number of occasions before becoming truly wild again. Put simply: when caged they would have been accustomed to humans coming near to them; for the first few months after being freed, they would probably not have been that bothered about being seen from a distance.

In fact, there were hardly any reported sightings across the whole country between 1976 and 1980. This explanation also ignores the nationwide sightings from the early 1960s onwards.

A more interesting explanation, and one that is not totally ridiculous, is the deliberate release either by some sort of 'mad scientist' to see how the animals would cope with the wild or by an extremist group with another agenda. There was a claim in February 2002 from a Scottish extremist group called the 'Rural Guerrillas' that they had released a number of lynx in Scotland as part of an operation to restore the original highland wildlife.

A slightly different story was heard by West Yorkshire Police when they seized two lynx a few years ago. The owner was planning on releasing them into the wild so that he and some friends could hunt them. Similar rumours, of lynx being released to be hunted, were circulating at the Game Fair at Shepton Mallet in 2002.

Some police forces have also had suggestions that certain major drug dealers are keeping big cats (illegally) as part of their 'hard image' and, in part, as security.

4. Non-physical entities or, to use a modern term, 'zooform phenomena'

Some people believe they are the ghosts of exotic cats that died in the area in the past and could not settle because they are so far from their natural home.

Another possibility, suggested by a university professor in California, is that humans may have an inherited tendency to interpret glimpsed predators as large cats. This could have developed in our evolutionary past as prehumans in Africa, when a species of large cat specialised in eating apes of our type. It was called *Dinofelis* and was one of the 'false' sabre-tooth cats. As a skilful hunter it was probably the 'predator to be most avoided'. Natural fear would have tended to make any sudden predator sighting into one of these large cats, and we might have inherited the tendency.

Such an explanation might fit a momentary sighting, but cannot apply when several witnesses see an animal together and watch it for some time or manage to photograph it.

Each explanation has its followers, and of course there may be different explanations for different cats.

The cats

Biologists divide the thirty-eight or so species of cat into two main groups: 'big cats' and 'small cats'. The division is based not really on size but more on throat structure. At a practical level it means that big cats can roar and small cats can purr. Basically the lion, tiger, leopard, jaguar and snow leopard are the big cats, and all the others are the small cats.

Typically the sightings of mystery big cats in England, Wales and Scotland fall under three descriptions.

The African leopard, not so far reported in Somerset. However its close relative the black panther has been sighted

1. 'Large black cat with a long tail'

Usually referred to as a black panther. The word panther in Europe tends to refer to the leopard (in the USA it can be the puma). The black panther is just a black form of leopard, and in the right light the spotted pattern can be seen in its black coat.

The leopard is the smallest of the true big cats, and in the wild still has one of the largest ranges of any cat. Its appearance, in both size and shades of coat, vary through its range.

The other large black cat which is sometimes seen in the wild is the jaguar. Although normally covered in rosettes, with coat colours similar to the leopard, the black jaguar occurs regularly enough to have been exhibited in captivity in the UK. Leopards have maintained their broad range in the wild partly by taking a wide range of prey.

2. 'Large brown cat with a long tail'

This is typically thought to be a puma, the largest of the small

A black leopard

cats in biological terms, and one of the most adaptable, having a massive range throughout the Americas. It is also a very secretive cat. Its diet in most of America is mainly deer, but it has survived by eating much smaller prey in areas where the deer were hunted out.

3. 'Large brown cat with a short tail or no tail'

Sometimes it has patterns in its coat, and the male may appear to have a mane – this would be a lynx, although there is a smaller North American species, known as the bobcat or bay lynx, which has a similar appearance. The lynx is smaller and stockier than the puma, and is currently found in parts of Europe, Asia and North America. Lynx will usually feed on rabbits, hares and, if they get the opportunity, small deer.

Each of the species described above, with the exception of the bobcat, has been imported into the UK in the past in relatively large numbers for exhibition in zoos and to some extent circuses. There has been the opportunity, therefore, for each species to escape or be released and to become established.

Having said that, black pumas are very unlikely to be here. Experts' opinions differ, but there have only ever been one or two seen in the Americas, none of which have been captured alive. No black puma has ever been imported into Britain. If one had, it would have been such a rarity that its escape, had it happened, would have made national news. Despite being regularly corrected, newspapers still persist in referring to sightings as being those of black pumas.

A puma still exists throughout continental America

The vast majority of sightings talked about in Somerset are of 'big black cats', although a number of pumas and one or two 'lynx-type' cats have also been reported. A number of species of exotic smaller cats have been found too – as 'road kill' or shot by farmers protecting their livestock. These are rarely reported prior to being killed, possibly because of their size: they can be mistaken for domestic dogs, cats or foxes. As far as I am aware, none of these smaller cats has ever been found in Somerset. Neighbouring counties, though, have yielded a leopard cat (Devon, 1988) and a jungle cat (Wiltshire, 1996).

The Somerset sightings are atypical in that, as well as witnesses of big black cats, there have also been people who are adamant they have seen a lion. Such claims are occasionally made in other parts of the country, but they are usually quickly resolved as misidentifications. That hasn't necessarily been so with the Somerset cases, although one suggested explanation would be that the 'lion' was in fact a misidentified puma. However if the witnesses truly saw a lion the only realistic explanation would be that it was an 'illegal' (i.e. unlicensed) pet which was out for only a short period of time before its owner recaptured it. If we genuinely had lions living wild in Great Britain the variety and size of prey being taken would make their presence very obvious.

Ecology

The Somerset environment should be well able to support a population of exotic cats. Large areas of woodland and open moors contain substantial populations of deer and rabbits as well as domestic livestock. Rabbits were introduced by the Normans, almost certainly after the lynx went extinct. In effect rabbits have no natural predator other than the fox, which takes a wide variety of other food. The two main species of deer (red and roe) are native and have always been managed as an asset for hunting. Populations of both rabbit and deer are now possibly under less control than they ever have been, and both are viewed, by many people at least, as major pests.

Exmoor's open moors and lonely woodlands provide an ideal habitat

A small group of exotic cats could make inroads into both deer and rabbit populations without any need to prey upon domestic livestock – but a cat will take what is available. Domestic livestock is occasionally attacked, and this is where the potential for major conflict with human beings occurs.

In fairness, the majority of sheep casualties are the result of dog attack, and it is remarkably difficult at times to tell the difference between a sheep that has been savaged by a dog and one that has been attacked by a large cat.

Generally, a dog will chase the whole herd, and may bite several sheep on their bottoms and back legs. If a sheep dies there will not be much meat missing from it, because the dog will typically be fed at home. Cat attacks, on the other hand, tend to involve a single animal being separated from the flock and being killed by damage to the head or neck (unfortunately, some dogs will also kill in this way). Typically up to 4-5 kg of meat will be missing from the prey animal if killed by a cat; more if it is feeding cubs. The body may also have been moved from where it was felled, and may even have been cached up a tree.

One of the confusing factors is that where bodies of deer or sheep remain overnight carrion feeders will come and remove much of the meat. Foxes in particular will feed on a carcass that they were not involved in killing. This may leave the body looking as if it is a predator kill, even if death was through natural causes.

In recent times the situation has become even more confused because of the training of lurchers for poaching deer, and the existence of the feral dog. Most rural police forces, even if they were to admit that wild big cats exist in their area, would probably agree that dogs pose a much greater risk to domestic livestock because they kill for fun and not just for food.

Brassknocker Hill Beasts

Brassknocker Hill is found in the parish of Monckton Combe just south of Bath. The hill is named after a house, originally a public house. It seems to have suffered from the short term visitations of a large number of diverse animals over the years in addition to mystery cats.

The area around the Combe Grove Hotel has often been the centre of these sightings. They first started in July 1979 when Ron and Betty Harper, who lived at Sun Cottage, had the bark stripped off the oak tree in their garden. Their goat was also badly frightened one night when the neighbours' cat disappeared and a dreadful scream was heard by several people at about 4.00 am. The cat later reappeared with a 18cm gash across its belly. The local newspaper dubbed whatever was wreaking havoc as the 'Beast of Bath'.

Tree damage continued throughout the area – by 1 August over thirty trees had been affected. It seemed to be mainly oaks, with a few beech trees included. Over the coming weeks several sightings occurred. Albert Miner of Bradford Road saw a 'strange animal' enter through a hole in his garden wall, leave through his garden gate, cross the road and disappear into the woods opposite. Although it was dusk, he could make out that it stood upright, was about two feet high [60cm], and was bushy and grey in colour.

On 9 August a three-man team led by Alan Heaslop of Combe Down spent several hours in the woods. During this time they saw a black creature swinging through the trees above them. When it dropped to the ground nearby and watched them, Alan dived and made a grab for it. Although he caught its leg, it screamed and pulled free. They described the animal as a chimpanzee, but then stated that it was 'about three feet [90cm] tall with a flat face and patches of grey and white on its chest'.

A local fisherman coming home late at night on a different day saw an animal which stood in the middle of the road. He thought that it was a baboon. This is just about possible as Longleat Safari Park, less than 20km south of Brassknocker Hill, had lost three baboons during an escape in February 1977.

The early 1980s brought a number of sightings of panther-like cats, some actually in the grounds of the Combe Grove Hotel. However, compared with other cat sightings none were particularly remarkable.

In the summer of 1984 there were further problems at Brassknocker Hill when the *Bath Chronicle* received reports of a strange animal holding up traffic in the road. Roger Green, the reporter who was sent to the scene, found the road to be clear so, with his photographer, Colin Shepheard, proceeded cautiously into the woods. After a few minutes searching they found the animal, calmly grazing in a field. It was an alpaca, a wool-producing domestic species closely related to the llama. The animal was subsequently taken into custody by the police and returned to the local lady who owned it.

There haven't been many reports of any sort of exotic animal sightings from Brassknocker Hill since the 1980s, but Batheaston, a village less than 8km to the north, has had some activity. The *Bath Chronicle* on 19 June 2003 reported that there had been a number of sightings of a big black cat in the area over the previous few weeks. It also reported that there had been a spate of cat sightings in the Batheaston area in 1988.

The Beast of Exmoor and the Beast of the Brendon Hills

At only 692k² (267 square miles) Exmoor is one of the smaller national parks in England. It has a small human population, and still has some remote, spacious open moorland and steep secretive wooded valleys.

To the east of it lie the Brendon Hills: these are heavily wooded at the north end but are divided into fields, often with beech hedges, to the south. The Brendon Hills have been described as the bridge between Exmoor proper and the Quantocks. As such they also provide a possible corridor for large cats and other animals to move discreetly from one major potential range to another. Both the Brendon Hills and Exmoor fall within the Exmoor National Park.

Although the Beast of Exmoor is normally considered to be an animal that lives/lived in Devon, there was a series of sightings in Somerset. The Beast of Exmoor story starts in the 1970s with a number of local reports. Large scale sheep kills began to occur on a farm at Drewstone near Barnstaple in 1982 and reports then crept into the national press. The following year further killings occurred, starting in March. The Royal Marines were called in to try to shoot the animal.

By late May it appeared to have moved into Somerset, with sheep kills reported at Simonsbath, Exford, Tarr Steps, Timberscombe and Brompton Regis. After a total of 78 days on the moor, interrupted by a withdrawal when large numbers of reporters made it dangerous to operate, the marines left. They claimed to have seen the animal or animals on a number of occasions, but each time were unable to take a 'safe shot' because of the background to the target(s). After this 'excursion' into Somerset the animal seems to have returned to north Devon, with subsequent reports of sheep killings being back there.

In late 1985 there were again sightings in Somerset, this time in the Minehead area. One family of four from Cardiff watched what they described as a 'big black cat' with a long curling tail running along a river bank near Hunters Inn.

The Lynx is a cat native to the British Isles. It became extinct in England before the Romans arrived, but small wild populations do still exist in parts of Europe

There was also a rather odd story concerning the disappearance of twenty pounds of tripe from the outbuildings at Woodcombe farm. A large footprint found nearby was identified by an expert engaged by a national newspaper as that of a wolverine. One of the local newspapers reported, with some satisfaction, that this was highly unlikely as the wolverine has five toes and the footprint had only four. The existence of wolverines in Great Britain in recent times is very unlikely, although reports are heard from time to time.

In May 1987 a large cat which looked like a puma was seen sunning itself on a hill near Timberscombe, in the Barle valley. The animal was observed for some time through binoculars, and this was an area where there had been sheep kills in 1983. In September of 1987 a large black cat was glimpsed crossing a forestry track at Luxborough on the Brendon Hills. The observer proceeded up the hill after catching sight of it, and within minutes found a heavily scratched log.

More recently, in 2000, another large cat was viewed just north of the National Park at Old Cleeve, near Watchet. A family saw the animal on three consecutive days.

For more details of the Beast of Exmoor see the books by Beer, Brierly and Francis in the further reading section on page 31.

The Quantocks

The Quantock Hills are supposed to contain some of the finest countryside in England. Indeed they were the first area to be awarded the status of an area of outstanding natural beauty (AONB) in 1956. Additionally the Quantock Common has been awarded legal protection as a Site of Special Scientific Interest (SSSI). The hills cover an area of some 19 km by 6 km and reach a maximum height of 386 m at Will's Neck.

The hilltops are largely covered by open heathland, but as one descends this rapidly gives way to broadleaved woodland, managed forest and farmland. Many valleys or combes cut into the hillsides and provide cover for wildlife. The three main encounters with large cats have all been on the eastern side of the Quantocks.

A number of sightings occurred at the end of July and the beginning of August 1994. An animal was first observed on 30 July on Bincombe Hill, near Over Stowey. Then on the morning of 31 July it was seen crossing the road between Goathurst and Broomfield. A day or two later it appeared near Hawkridge reservoir.

The *Western Morning News* of 28 November 1994 carried a report of a sighting by voluntary hill warden Terry Moran who had seen, and photographed, what he thought may have been a puma. At the time he was walking his collie Jess at Holcombe Combe, about 400 m from Holford village. Mr Moran saw the animal walking away from him, up the hill, before it disappeared into the undergrowth. He had a camera with him to photograph the local waterfalls after the recent rain. Unfortunately the lens was only 70 mm, so the picture was not very detailed – although because it was taken through a wire fence it did give some indication of the cat's size. Through his work as a warden Mr Moran had heard of a big cat having been sighted in the Quantocks previously.

These sightings should also be considered together with those in the Bridgwater area, because Bridgwater is only 8 km from the southern end of the Quantocks.

One further note of interest. At Watchet there is a small tourist attraction called Tropiquaria at the former BBC transmitting station. The main part of the attraction is the old transmitter hall which is now a wonderful tropical house containing exotic plants and animals. In the early days of its operation the owners employed the late Clive Bennett as their senior keeper. Clive had an almost encyclopaedic knowledge of animals and a long history in the zoo world, having originally trained at Belle Vue Zoo in Manchester.

When I visited Tropiquaria in 1998 I had a long talk with Clive about various exotic animals locally. I was particularly interested in sightings of wallabies at the time because there had been some recent escapes in the Exmoor area.

Clive, quite out of the blue, said something which came as a surprise. Apparently there had been a number of sightings of what several people had described as a strange cat that was too big to be a domestic in the north part of the Quantock Hills. He had spoken to several witnesses and discovered that the animal was a civet cat! Despite its name the civet is not in fact a cat but a Vivverid, a (large) member of the mongoose family.

A civet would almost certainly be capable of surviving in the Quantocks, or almost anywhere else in the United Kingdom, but it is difficult to imagine how it might have got there as few have ever been imported.

Beasts around Bridgwater

Bridgwater is a small river port town on the river Parrett which has proved popular with Somerset's mystery cats over the years.

Towards the end of 1992 one of the more alarming incidents in the history of big cats in the county occurred when a car containing several people was allegedly attacked. A 'big black cat like thing with huge teeth' sprang at the Citroen being driven by Susan Stretch on a quiet lane through Cossington, near Bridgwater.

The car contained Mrs Stretch, her three children and Lyn Wardell, a friend, and her two children. Mrs Wardell said the animal was baring its teeth as it charged towards the car.

When she saw the cat in the headlights, Mrs Stretch braked hard to avoid hitting it. She expected it to run away, but instead it charged and threw itself against the side of the car. It hit the car with such a thump that Mrs Stretch thought it might have been killed. In fact it wasn't. According to the *Western Morning News* of 16 December this was the third sighting of the cat in the area 'within recent weeks'.

Another sighting that was reported from this general area happened in February 1994 when Phil Gamblin saw what he described as a 'huge black cat with a long tail' in Love Lane, Burnham. However he added that he wouldn't say that it was as big as a panther.

A year later, on 7 August 1995, Wayne Broad was in his garden in Pawlett, north of Bridgwater, when he thought he saw a fox in the next field. He dashed inside to find his video camera. When he focused on the animal he was surprised to discover that it was a 'six foot long' (1.8m) cat-like creature with a sweeping tail that was prowling through the newly harvested field. The animal reappeared two days later, on the 9th. Wayne later borrowed a neighbour's domestic cat and filmed it in the same place, from the same distance. This animal could barely be seen above the stubble, and confirmed the large size of the first cat.

Later sightings include one by two policemen who saw a large cat at Enmore, near Bridgwater, in June 1998. Another cat was

The leopard cat is a species of wild cat from eastern Asia. It has been hybridised with the domestic cat

spotted at Puriton on 16 March 2003 – it was photographed in a field near the village by a local woman. She described the animal as being black and about the size of a labrador.

Taunton and the Blackdown Hills

Taunton is a market town and the administrative headquarters of the county of Somerset. It is situated to the north of the Blackdown Hills, in a valley on the river Tone. Sightings in this area started in about 1993 when John Tutton described a 'black puma type cat' crossing the Taunton road at Corfe early one morning. The animal was seen again in late August. Then in mid-November of the same year it was claimed that male and female panthers were together in a field at Orchard Portman. The male was estimated as being about 28 inches [71cm] tall and weighing about 120 pounds [54 kilos].

The *Western Daily Press* reported on 8 June 2000 that a female puma and litter of cubs could be living within a few miles of the centre of Taunton near Churchinford. Local chef Sophie Stevens saw the adult as she drove her children to school in Wellington. She described it as being at least 4¹/₂ feet [1.35m] long in the body, with a tail that was probably another 2¹/₂ feet [0.75m] long. It was fawn in colour, but appeared almost white in the bright sunlight. After dropping the children at school Mrs Stevens returned to the area and found a dead, almost fully grown roe deer. She then fetched her brother, and on their return the body had been dragged further away and more of it had been eaten.

After collecting the children from school Mrs Stevens continued to explore the area and discovered that the deer carcass had been dragged even further from where she had first found it. It was now lying next to a large drain running under the road. In this drain were also the remains of another deer. About a month earlier a puma had been seen early in the morning, sitting by the roadside in the same area.

Further sightings occurred throughout the following years, but they were usually not so clear. A typical example was that on 20 July 2003: a car driver and passenger were travelling through the Blackdown Hills, 25 km from Taunton on the Honiton Road, and were passing through what they described as wooded farmland when they saw an animal 'the size of a pig', but moving 'in a cat-like manner'. Although it was dark, both the driver and passenger were agreed that it was not black, but a 'light brown colour'.

The sightings in 1993 of a big black cat to the south west of Taunton – at Corfe and Orchard Portman as described above – stopped as suddenly as they had started. The records of the Dorset big cat group reveal that a year later, in September 1994, reports began to appear of what the press called 'the beast of Broadwindsor'. Witnesses all claimed to have spotted a black cat as large as an Alsatian dog. Since then there have been an increasing number of big black cat sightings around the four Dorset villages of Broadwindsor, Beaminster, Melplash and Netherbury. As the distance from Corfe to Broadwindsor is less than 30 km and there are no major rivers or motorways to cross, this could be the same animal and/or its descendants.

The Monster of the Mendips, the Shipham Panther, the Churchill Lion or the Coleford Cat?

The Mendip Hills are situated to the north of the Somerset Levels. They are about 30 km long and range from 5-10 km wide, with a gently undulating central plateau much of which is used for agriculture. Around the edges of the plateau there is a lot of woodland, some of which is of ancient origin. The slopes, particularly to the north and south, are interspersed with dry valleys and gorges which give potential cover for wildlife. The majority of the reported sightings seem to divide into two main groups: to the south and east of the hills, and a band that crosses and caps the northern end of the Mendips.

Reports start in about 1993, when the Plymouth-based *Evening Herald* states in a list of cat sightings, 'two separate people see a Puma in the Mendips'. No further discussion or details are given. This report probably relates to a sighting by Glyn Morgan at Whatley, near Frome, in late July. The same, or a similar animal, had occasionally been seen during the previous few weeks in the area by a number of people, but they didn't report it until after the Whatley sighting. Most descriptions were of a light brown animal about 1.5m long with a 60cm tail.

In February of the following year at the village of Gurney Slade, just south east of the hills, Roger Snook had a surprise when he went into his garden shed and a big cat hurtled past him. The animal jumped over the garden wall. He saw it again an hour later at the bottom of the garden. It was thought that it may have sheltered overnight in the shed because of the adverse weather. An RSPCA inspector later attended the scene with a tracker dog. They found large tracks leading into the local woods, but the dog was unable or unwilling to follow the scent any further.

There seem to have been no other reports from this area at this time, but the following summer, 30 km to the south at

Motcombe, just across the border in Dorset, there were a number of sightings of what became known as the 'Motcombe Beast'. Loud yowling noises were also heard there over several months, and at least one good set of cat footprints was found.

Sightings occur in the Gurney Slade area again in September 2002: Jane Rous-Milligan saw what she described as a 'big black animal' walk across the bottom of her Holcombe garden at about 4pm one afternoon. Holcombe is 5km from Gurney Slade. The next sighting to be reported came in February 2003 when Sue Mattick at Leigh-upon-Mendip (about 8km from Gurney Slade) saw a big black cat. Then in January 2004 a farmer from Stoke St Michael suffered a series of attacks on his sheep and cows by a cat-like animal. Three months later five men driving through Leigh-upon-Mendip in the evening narrowly missed hitting a big cat. They could only really describe it as being dark in colour and having large bright yellow eyes.

In March of 2004 the *Wells Journal* reported that a woman walking her dog in Wookey had seen a large black cat only yards away from her. June Edwards saw the animal at about 3.45pm while walking her dog Molly: the dog and the cat ran parallel to each other in a field before the cat turned away and went towards Yarley. Wookey is about 12km west of Gurney Slade.

The next major sighting from this area comes from Hilary Corner who on 4 August 2004 was walking her pet Doberman 'Anya' in the Common Lane area between Holcombe and Coleford. The dog disappeared momentarily and when it returned it was carrying a deer haunch in its mouth. Shortly afterwards she noticed that the dog was watching something in the distance. When she looked where the dog was peering, she saw a 'large, healthy, shiny cat with big hips turn away from the carcass of a deer and run up a tree'. She stated that it was jet-black in colour, about five feet [1.5m] long, not including the tail, and was moving like a puma or a large wild cat. Mrs Corner was aware of several other people from the village who had spotted a similar animal in the preceding month.

The report in the Frome and *Somerset Guardian* led to a number of other locals contacting the newspaper with previously

African lions at home, the male standing, a female lying down. Unlike other cats they are sociable. Was one really seen at Churchill, 5 km north of Cheddar, in 2001?

unreported sightings. Possibly as a result of a journalistic liking for alliteration, this animal became known as the 'Coleford Cat', Coleford being a village in the middle of the cluster of sightings.

In 2001 the 'Churchill Lion' sighting was notable for two reasons. Firstly, the initial suggestion that a lion was involved piqued people's curiosity, and secondly the main sighting involved a relatively large number of witnesses. It also coincided with a series of sightings at the north end of the Mendips, which subsequently were linked with some earlier and later observations in the Chew Valley area.

The Rowberrow service station is on the A38 on the northern edge of the Mendip Hills, near Churchill in north Somerset. On Friday 17 August 2001 Susan Todd, who had stopped to buy petrol, spotted what she thought was a lioness in the fields on the hillside opposite. At least half a dozen other motorists also stopped to watch the animal as it walked across the fields and then disappeared into the woods. The station manageress, Susan Rodgers, saw it too and quickly asked the motorists if anybody had binoculars. Unfortunately in the heat of the moment she forgot that the service station stocked disposable cameras!

In all about a dozen witnesses saw the animal. The police arrived after it had disappeared and their subsequent search revealed nothing. For one excited witness, Steve Phillips, it was his second big cat sighting. His first had occurred a year earlier when he watched a big cat from the bedroom window of his Blagdon home.

Just over a week later Mike Hanford was driving his car near Ubley, about six miles [9.5 km] to the west of Churchill, when he saw a light tan cat in a field. He described the size as 'bigger than a pig but not quite so big as a Shetland pony'. With the village of Blagdon being nearby, the animal quickly became the 'Beast of Blagdon'.

Possibly the most interesting sighting in 2003 happened in September. Two workers on the night shift at Callow Quarry, near Shipham, saw at close range what they described as a black panther. Brian Webb glimpsed the animal first and put out a call on his radio. His colleague Richard Smith, thinking that it was a joke, went over to where Brian was working and realised it was no joke at all. Both were agreed that it definitely was a panther, as it 'was far too big for anything else'. They immediately reported their experience to the police. In fact local police sergeant Paul Knowles had seen a similar animal six years previously a short distance away at Axbridge, when out on patrol.

Mark Hill, a supermarket manager from Cheddar, had a surprise when he was driving through the Mendip Hills on a Monday in June 2004. As he passed Wigmore Farm on the road between Priddy and Chewton Mendip, he saw a large black cat 'like a panther' in the middle of the road, eating from a discarded fish and chip wrapper. The animal was apparently unconcerned at his presence, even though he was only a metre or so from it. It continued to eat from the wrapper for about a minute and a half before moving off. In the report in the *Cheddar Valley Gazette* mention was also made of the fact that cavers had found the remains of an animal which appeared to have been recently torn apart by a large predator in caves at Priddy.

Just north of the Mendips there is a natural valley system which contains two lakes, Blagdon Lake and Chew Valley Lake. This area has also been a hot spot for cat sightings, and there is no reason not to believe that an animal living in the Mendips could also extend its range in this direction. Sightings here started in about 1998: in May a light brown coloured cat about 60-90cm tall was seen at Wrington. A month later another cat was seen at Felton near Bristol airport.

In August 2001, on the same day as the 'lion' sighting near Churchill, a dead and mutilated sheep was found at Robert Harding's farm at Winford. It was the fourth sheep that Mr Harding had lost in this way since the previous October. He had farmed at Spring Farm, Winford, for 40 years and believed that these four sheep kills were different from those he had previously seen.

In each of the four cases the rest of the flock had not been distressed for days after, as they often are with dog attacks. He also described the sheep's injuries as having required a very powerful animal to inflict them.

Just over a week after the Winford sheep killing Mike Hanford saw a cat at Ubley, between the two lakes. Ubley and Winford are 7 km apart. A few months later, in early November 2001, Robert Harding's other farm, Valley View Farm in Dundry, had three sheep killed and partly eaten in a week. Although an experienced farmer and butcher, he had never seen damage quite like that before. He built a wire cage trap in which he hoped to catch the animal responsible. It is assumed that as yet he has been unsuccessful.

It is difficult to try to interpret the North Mendip sightings, as there are reports of a black cat, a brown cat and a lion. If we assume that the lion was in fact a puma, it would seem that there is or has been both a puma and a black leopard in the area.

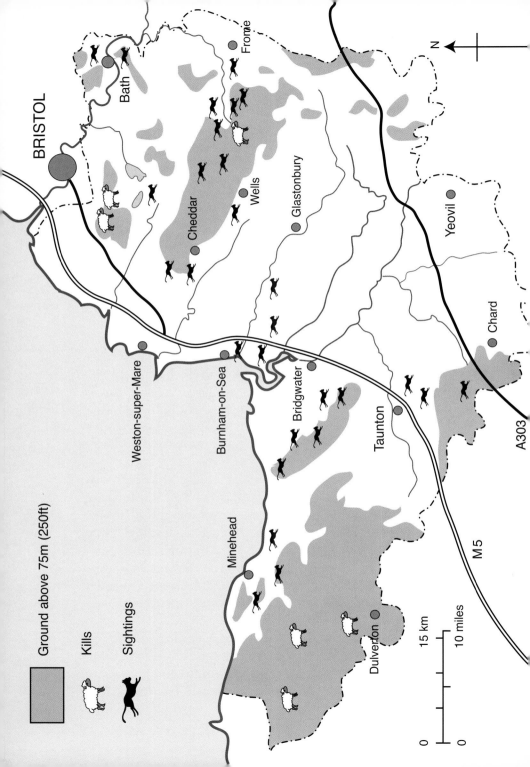

N

BRISTOL

Bath

Frome

Cheddar

Wells

Glastonbury

Yeovil

Weston-super-Mare

Burnham-on-Sea

Bridgwater

Chard

Taunton

Minehead

Dulverton

A303

M5

Ground above 75m (250ft)

Kills

Sightings

15 km

10 miles

0

0

Catwatching

If the Somerset sightings are marked on a map, it becomes obvious that certain places are cat 'hotspots'. So anybody who wants to see a cat should naturally concentrate on them – in recent times the area to the south east of the Mendips would seem to be worth a look, as would the Chew Valley lake area and the Callow Quarry area near Shipham. Other parts of the county seem not to be favoured by the cats at all and therefore spending any time watching there is likely to be wasted.

However, the real chances of seeing a large cat are, frankly, poor. Each of the cat species that have been suggested as being in the county are capable of moving 30 km in a night and may regularly cover a range of 50 km² or more.

They are also incredibly secretive: they have to be to be successful predators. In America several states are currently discovering that they have pumas, when they thought that the puma had disappeared when the deer were hunted out, often a hundred years ago. The pumas are generally thought to be surviving populations rather than recent re-introductions or immigrants. All species of cat also have a sense of smell that is 1-2 million times better than that of a human and they have excellent vision too. These super-senses are necessary for them to survive as predators, but they also enable the cat to avoid people.

If you are planning on taking pictures with a view to selling them, it's best to use a conventional camera with film. The photographs are less easy to tamper with than digital images and the chances of being accused of faking the images are reduced. If you are hoping to sell the pictures, but are concerned for the animal's welfare, then delay passing them to the press for a few days to allow the animal to move out of the area. Additionally, ask the paper to remove any features in the picture that identify the exact location.

As large predators, big cats are potentially dangerous and should only be watched from a distance. The general rule, and this applies to watching any large wild animal, is that it is best to

A map of Somerset showing the big cat sightings discussed in this book

avoid approaching it directly. If it approaches you, do *not* run away as this may provoke an automatic chase response in a predator. It is thought that several attacks in the United States occurred because joggers ran past pumas, not knowing they were there. Once a jogger runs away from it, a puma will go into 'automatic pilot' – it will begin a chase and will ultimately bring a person down.

If an animal does move towards you, make yourself look as big as possible – wave your arms around above your head – and create a lot of noise. If you are blocking its obvious escape route move slowly out of the way, without turning away from it. Also bear in mind that domestic farm livestock can be dangerous and that in areas where there are deer there may also be people hunting with rifles.

There is one other general rule about field biology, which is that no matter how many books you may have read on animal behaviour, or the behaviour of the species you are watching, the 'rules' are generalisations and may not be followed by the individual animal in front of you.

The future

If the cats that we are considering are the descendants of animals released when the Dangerous Wild Act came into force in 1976, then they must now be in the third or fourth generation, at least. If this is the case, and as they are seen more frequently than they were in the 1970s, then they must be approaching a stable and viable population. Subject to there not being a sudden epizootic (animal version of an epidemic) of cat disease, the population should continue to expand slowly.

An expanding population will lead to even more sightings and, potentially, greater conflict with domestic livestock. The positive side is that larger numbers of predators will have a greater impact on rabbits and deer. As controls on hunting with dogs and firearm possession become tighter, there is a potential for the deer and rabbit populations to surge out of control and cause serious economic damage to crop production. As a means of controlling this damage, more big cats would have obvious benefits.

Generally the cats do seem to attract public sympathy. In Devon there was a report of a lion being seen at a place called Wrangaton in late 1998 and early 1999. The police turned up in large numbers with firearms and the force helicopter was called in. Their official statement implied they did not intend to shoot as a matter of first resort, but if there was a safety issue they would pull the trigger. At the time there were no local reports of livestock attacks, and none of the witnesses felt threatened (they were all in cars). Local gossip in one of the pubs over the next few weeks indicated that many residents would not report sightings in case it led to the police killing the animal.

When a new hunting magazine was published in late 2003/early 2004 it offered a £1000 prize for the first person to present it with the corpse of a British big cat that had been lawfully shot. This caused several protests, and probably attracted the media attention the editor, Charlie Jacoby, wanted for his new magazine. He stood by his offer, despite criticism from the British Big Cat Society and the RSPCA. *The Taunton Times* carried a report about it early in January and, coincidentally, later in the month stated that a Cranmore farmer was waiting by bait with a shotgun for whatever was killing his livestock. In the previous two weeks he had lost four adult ewes and a six month old Aberdeen Angus calf to a mystery predator.

The danger to humans posed by big cats, however, seems currently to be slight. Although there have been a number of alleged attacks (none, at the time of writing, in Somerset), none have been fatal, and the majority happened under questionable circumstances. In most instances the victims' injuries are clearly incompatible with the claims: generally they are suspiciously trivial when compared with the size of the claws and teeth on lynx, puma and leopard.

Possibly the two most convincing claims, where the victims both have substantial scarring, happened when they deliberately approached the animal. In one case, in the Midlands, a churchyard had been baited for some time to attract the local big cat.

The person attacked went to see the bait and, not realising the cat was there, was knocked out of the way as it escaped. The injuries resulted from a single swipe with the paw. The other incident, in East Anglia, involved a man attempting to rescue a domestic rabbit from the mouth of what he thought was a fox, but when he got closer it appeared to be a lynx. He suffered one paw swipe across the back of the hand.

Conclusions

The sightings and other evidence referred to in this book suggest that a number of large cat territories exist in Somerset. Whilst a few sightings have been reported from outside these areas, the bulk have occurred from within them. Even if some are discredited as hoaxes or mistakes, there is still a group of believable reports by responsible people that are strongly indicative of the existence of a population of puma or black leopard.

The territories seem to contain, in many cases, a virtually ideal habitat for the animals and they are sufficiently large to produce enough wildlife to feed a big solitary predator such as a puma or leopard without it needing to take domestic livestock regularly. Where domestic livestock is taken as prey, the numbers are generally insignificant compared with the fatalities that occur through dog attack, poor husbandry, climatic effects and natural causes.

With possibly the majority of people wanting them to remain unharmed, the animals are becoming part of the folklore of the county too. A good example of the way this is happening was described in a report about local artist James Lynch in the *Western Gazette* in August 2003. Mr Lynch had produced a number of paintings of Somerset big cats, and they were being exhibited at the Maas gallery in London. He said that they were inspired by reading reports of the animals in the local papers, although he did have a friend who had actually seen a beast in a field.

The only people opposed to the presence of the cats seem to

be those who have lost domestic livestock to them, or are worried about public safety. The safety angle still needs a proper assessment, if that is possible. As yet it seems there have been no human fatalities that are known of. Where there are claims of attacks on humans, they tend either to be not convincing or the 'victim' deliberately approached the cat.

To put it in context, people die every year as a result of contact with cattle, deer, bees and wasps.

If a particular animal was to become a nuisance, either through regular livestock attacks or a human attack, it is likely that attempts would be made to shoot it. Some farmers in the county have already tried live-trapping using cage traps, but as far as we know without success.

Cage traps do work, though. Ted Noble, a farmer in Scotland, caught a puma in 1980 using a cage trap, and a leopard cat was caught in the Isle of Wight in 1987 in the same way. A Somerset puma or black panther caught in the wild would almost certainly be of some value to any zoological garden or exotic animal refuge that was to take it in because of the number of visitors it would attract. In such a case local businesses might be willing to enter into sponsorship arrangements to pay for the animal's upkeep.

Further reading

There are no books which deal specifically, in detail, with the mystery cats of Somerset. However, there are three books (numbers one, two and four on the list) that consider the beast of Exmoor, although they do tend to look at the subject from a Devon perspective. Two at least are out of print, but they can often be picked up from secondhand bookshops.

Beer, Trevor, *The Beast of Exmoor: Fact or legend?* (Countryside Productions, Barnstaple, 1988)

Brierly, Nigel, *They stalk by night – the big cats of Exmoor and the South West* (Yeo Valley Productions, Bishops Nympton, 1988)

Downes, Jon, *The smaller mystery carnivores of the Westcountry* (CFZ, Exeter, 1996)

Francis, Di, *The Beast of Exmoor and other mystery predators of Britain* (Jonathan Cape, London, 1993)

Moiser, Chris, *Mystery cats of Devon and Cornwall* (Bossiney Books, Launceston, 2001)

Shuker, Karl, *Mystery cats of the world* (Robert Hale, London, 1989)

For up to date information, local newspapers often carry reports of sightings, domestic livestock kills and other evidence. Many also have websites which will provide a search for the last six months through a group of newspapers, not just a single title. The *Western Morning News*, the *Western Daily Press* and the *Sunday Independent* all seem to like cat stories and do carry them as space permits.

The British Big Cat Society (motto: 'to prove and protect') and the Exeter-based Centre for Fortean Zoology both have websites which give frequent updates on sightings. Two magazines also carry regular reports: these are Animals and Men, produced by the Centre for Fortean Zoology, and the Fortean Times, a nationally produced magazine which looks at strange phenomena generally, but which does occasionally produce a year's 'round up' of big cat sightings. There is also a Dorset big cat group which has a website and reports some 'across the border' sightings in Somerset.